Proven Strategies That Work for Teaching Gifted & Advanced Learners

for Grades 3–8

Proven Strategies That Work for Teaching Gifted & Advanced Learners

Kathleen McConnell Fad, Ph.D., and Gail Ryser, Ph.D.

NEW YORK AND LONDON

First published in 2015 by Prufrock Press Inc.

Published in 2021 by Routledge
605 Third Avenue, New York, NY 10017
2 Park Square, Milton Park, Abingdon, Oxon OX14 4RN

Routledge is an imprint of the Taylor & Francis Group, an informa business.

Cover design by Raquel Trevino and layout design by Allegra Denbo

ISBN: 9781032141565 (hbk)
ISBN: 9781618214041 (pbk)

DOI: 10.4324/9781003237389

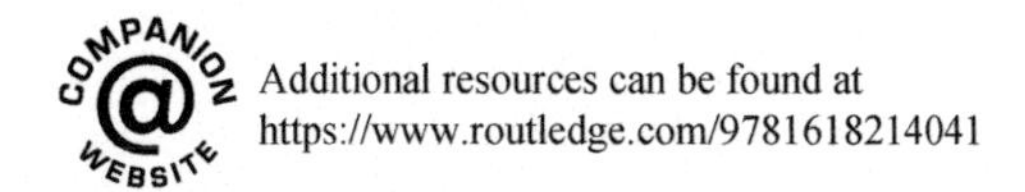

Additional resources can be found at
https://www.routledge.com/9781618214041

TABLE OF CONTENTS

INTRODUCTION

We created *Proven Strategies That Really Work for Teaching Gifted and Advanced Learners* for educators who work with advanced learners. The term "advanced learners" is commonly used to describe students who are performing at high levels of accomplishment. Many advanced learners are identified as gifted and talented (GT) students, while others may not be identified but demonstrate many of the same characteristics. The book provides teachers with strategies that can be implemented both in mixed-ability or cluster-grouped classrooms, as well as homogeneously grouped GT classes. The strategies are designed for students in grades 3–8.

Before writing the strategies, we identified three key areas of importance to educators: assessment, content, and instruction (including acceleration of learning). The literature has consistently supported differentiation of instruction for students who are advanced learners, and these three areas are commonly identified as pathways to differentiation. There are already many formats for differentiation that are well-established and effective models for use with advanced learners. Among them are curriculum compacting (Reis, Burns, & Renzulli, 1992; Renzulli & Reis, 1998), tiered objectives and choices/menus (Tomlinson, 2014), project-based learning (Stanley, 2012), and others. *Proven Strategies That Really Work for Teaching Gifted and Advanced Learners* does not include those differentiation techniques because we believe that they are already widely used and supported by numerous references in the literature and are readily available for teachers.

Instead, *Proven Strategies That Really Work for Teaching Gifted and Advanced Learners* provides new strategies that can be used immediately by teachers. We assume that the teachers working with advanced learners have a clear understanding of the characteristics of students who are gifted and talented, a background in the fundamentals of differentiation, and thorough professional development experiences that have included the differentiation models mentioned above. We did not think that repeating differentiation models that are already widely disseminated is as helpful as providing original, classroom-ready strategies that teachers can integrate into their planned instruction.

The book is not intended as a textbook, but rather is designed for educators who are looking for strategies they can implement quickly and easily while still meeting the needs of their advanced learners. Because so many school districts now use cluster grouping or other models that integrate GT students into general education classrooms with other nongifted students, teachers may struggle to differentiate for their most advanced learners. Planning for differentiation and then implementing it in diverse classrooms requires knowledge, time, and expertise. We believe that this book can be helpful in supporting teachers as they do this important work. For educators who work with advanced learners, these materials should become a basic, "go-to" resource.

The strategies in this book encompass a wide variety of topics. The accompanying forms and reproducibles are user-friendly resources designed to help teachers maximize their stu-dents' learning. The forms and reproducibles can be accessed on the routledge Press website at http://www.routledge.com/Assets/ClientPages/Proven_Strategies.aspx. Teachers may use the materials for their students and have permission to share materials for single-class-room use.

The three domains addressed by the strategies include:

- assessment,
- content, and
- instruction (including acceleration of learning).

We will briefly describe the three areas of differentiation.

Assessment consists of activities that yield information that can be used for placement, programming decisions, and monitoring student progress (Johnsen, Ryser, & Assouline, 2014). Assessments can be formal or informal and take place at the beginning, during, or end of instruction. For advanced and gifted learners, it is important to preassess to determine if the student has mastered some of the content before instruction has begun. Formative assessment is also important to determine students' depth of understanding (Sheffield, 2000).

Content consists of the major ideas, concepts, facts, and skills related to an area of study (Berger, 1991). Furthermore, content is what we want students to know and understand. Teachers organize and sequence content within and across disciplines. Organizing and sequencing content at a high level of differentiation implies that student performance and interest guide the organization of the content (Johnsen, Haensly, Ryser, & Ford, 2002). Content can be differentiated using a variety of methods, including compacting, adding depth and complexity, using flexible pacing, increasing abstractness, and organizing around major themes and ideas.

Instruction is the manner in which we deliver content to students. Effective curriculum models for advanced or gifted learners favor an inquiry-based model of instruction and promote providing instruction at an accelerated rate (VanTassel-Baska & Brown, 2007). In addition, instruction should be adjusted in response to students' readiness, interest, and learning profiles (Tomlinson et al., 2003).

Four-Step Preassessment

Strategy Target

- Assessment

Purpose

Before advanced learners begin independent study, individual contracts, independent research, or in-class acceleration strategies, it is critical to preassess their knowledge. There are many ways to preassess. Some are very thorough and others provide a quick, more general overview of student knowledge. Preassessments can be formal, written assessments or they can be informal, verbal, or demonstration type assessments.

This preassessment strategy is a four-step assessment. It is similar to other strategies that break down learning objectives (Heacox, 2009). If you find the form included with this strategy useful (see the Four-Step Preassessment form at the end of this section), we suggest that you create an electronic, interactive template of it and use it to preassess students before teaching a unit of instruction or a series of lessons. It is not as useful for preassessing discrete skills taught in one individual lesson.

Process

To use the four-step preassessment (see the example in Figure 1), use the following steps:

1. Review the objective and goals for your next unit of instruction and write them at the top of the form along with the students' name.
2. Write the preassessment during the planning process and *before* teaching the unit. Teachers must know what vocabulary and facts are critical to student understanding. Teachers also must be very clear about the overall theme, principle, or concept that they want students to master. Finally, in order to make sure students meet objectives, teachers should design some tasks, activities, and/or assignments that will demonstrate student learning.

Name: Student

Date: January 21

FOUR-STEP PREASSESSMENT

Before beginning a unit of instruction or a series of lessons on the same topic, use this form to determine the student's level of mastery of the content.

Topic: The legislative process

Objective/Goals: To understand how a bill becomes a law in the U.S.

Assessment Step	Teacher Question	Student Response	Date
Vocabulary	In your own words, tell what these words mean: 1. Resolution 2. Constituents 3. Veto	1. 2. 3.	
Facts	Answer these questions about the topic: 1. How does a bill get introduced? 2. What does it mean for a bill to be enrolled? 3. What happens to a bill if the President vetoes it?	1. 2. 3.	
Understanding	Explain the key theme, principle, or concept related to this topic by answering this question, explaining verbally, or demonstrating. Question: How does a bill become law in the U.S.?		
Demonstration	Complete these tasks to demonstrate your understanding (above): 1. Flow chart of steps. 2. Describe three options of the President's actions. 3.	1. 2. 3.	

FIGURE 1. Four-step preassessment example.

3. After making all of the instructional decisions described in Step 2, complete the teacher portion of the Four-Step Preassessment form. The four sections indicated are Vocabulary, Facts, Understanding, and Demonstration.
4. Provide students with the preassessment and have them respond in the Student Response Column or allow for verbal responses, demonstrations, or product evaluations.
5. If the students are able to demonstrate mastery of everything on the Four-Step Preassessment, they can proceed with independent work, research, alternate assignments, or in-class acceleration. If students fail to master only a small portion of the learning required, then allow for targeted activities before they proceed on their own.

FOUR-STEP PREASSESSMENT

Name:____ Date: ________________

Before beginning a unit of instruction or a series of lessons on the same topic, use this form to determine the student's level of mastery of the content.

Topic: ____

Objective/Goals: ____

Assessment Step	Teacher Question	Student Response	Date
Vocabulary	In your own words, tell what these words mean: 1. 2. 3.	1. 2. 3.	
Facts	Answer these questions about the topic: 1. 2. 3.	1. 2. 3.	
Understanding	Explain the key theme, principle, or concept related to this topic by answering this question, explaining verbally, or demonstrating. Question:		
Demonstration	Complete these tasks to demonstrate your understanding (above): 1. 2. 3.	1. 2. 3.	

Preassess With a Topic Web

Strategy Targets

- Instruction
- Assessment

Purpose

To preassess the whole class before starting a new unit of instruction or topic, use a group topic web. Although this strategy may be supplemented with additional information gathered individually, it is a great way to start the preassessment process. Getting feedback from the whole class allows teachers to quickly determine which students' responses indicate divergent, original, and/or fluent thinking.

This activity should provide any teacher with information about students' prior knowledge related to a specific topic. The next step for preassessment could be to follow up with the students who provided unique, detailed, or high-level information, as well as those students who had many ideas to share and were very confident. If a student already knows what is about to be taught, then alternate assignments that include extension or enrichment should be used.

Process

Group topic webs have been used often in classrooms. Heacox (2009) and others have provided examples of how a topic web can be used effectively. This strategy is simple, yet effective, for classes that use cluster grouping to serve advanced learners. A sample completed topic web (Figure 1) and a Group Topic Web Form are provided at the end of the section. Just follow these steps:

1. To introduce a new topic and find out how much students know, create an open topic web for the whole group. In the middle of a whiteboard or large piece of chart

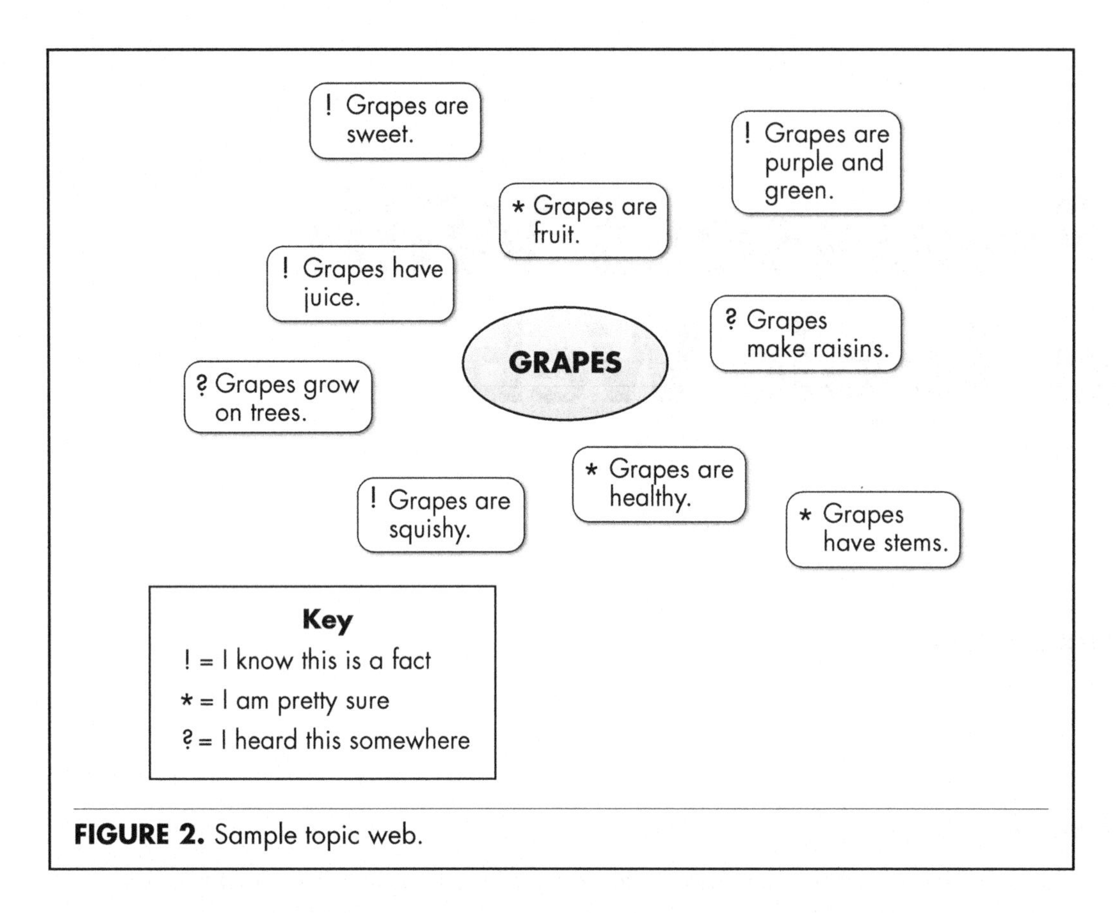

FIGURE 2. Sample topic web.

paper, write the key word for the new unit. This key word can be as simple as the topic.

2. Before beginning discussion, ask students to tell what they already know about this topic. Ask students to write just a few words or a simple phrase. They can either come to the whiteboard a few at a time or write on sticky notes if you are using chart paper.
3. In addition to writing the information that they already know, ask students to code their information this way:
   - Use an exclamation point if they are confident that what they are writing is a fact.
   - Use an asterisk if they are just pretty sure that what they are writing is fact.
   - Use a question mark if they are not sure about the information. They can still offer ideas, but ask them to let you know if they *think* something is a fact or if they are not 100% sure.

4. Ask students to write their initials next to their idea on the whiteboard or on the back of the sticky note if using paper/pencil.
5. After students have each contributed three to five ideas, ask small groups to organize the information into sections. Give each group about 5 minutes to organize the sticky notes or whiteboard comments. At first, do not give students too much guidance. Watch to see how they organize the information on their own.
6. Record which students provide accurate information during this activity. Also make note of whether students were confident that their ideas were correct.

GROUP TOPIC WEB FORM

Topic/Unit: ______________________________

Student	Did the student contribute at least one idea that was original, unique, or interesting? Yes/No	Did the student contribute several ideas? Yes/No	Was the student confident that his contributions were accurate? Yes/No

GROUP TOPIC WEB FORM

Self-Check
Show Me or Tell Me

Strategy Target

- Assessment

Purpose

If teachers want their advanced learners to master high-level learning tasks, students should learn to self-assess and set goals for themselves. By self-checking and demonstrating mastery of learning targets, students who are gifted and talented can confidently move on to enrichment activities, including independent work, self-paced instruction, project-based learning, and learning contract tasks.

Demonstrating knowledge on teacher-designed assessments usually involves answering close-ended, convergent questions. The Self-Check: Show Me or Tell Me form at the end of this section provides a strategy that teachers can use to teach (see Figure 3 for an example completed form). Students can also use the form to assess their own learning and use the information to set a new personal learning target. This process can be used as a preassessment at the beginning of a unit of instruction or to assess a specific objective embedded in a unit.

Process

To provide instruction and guide your advanced learners as they self-assess and set goals, follow these steps:

1. After reviewing your curriculum and the goals and objectives you will be teaching, decide on a specific learning target that you want students to master.
2. Discuss this learning target, and on the self-assessment form, write it as a first-person statement for the student, using "I can" to begin the statement. (For example, "I can explain what happens during the water cycle, including condensation and evaporation.")

Name: Student Date: April 5

SELF-CHECK: SHOW ME OR TELL ME

As your teacher directs, complete this form to show that you already understand the information about to be taught. Then plan ahead to go further in your learning.

Topic or Objective: The water cycle

Learning Target:

I can: explain what happens during the water cycle, including evaporation and condensation.

I will Show You/Tell You. (Check one)

❑ To *show you* I can meet the learning target, here is my evidence (or see attached):

____

____

____

____

____

✔ I will *tell you* what I need to in order to meet the learning target. Please let me know when it is convenient to tell you what I have learned.

My next goal related to this topic or objective is to show or tell you that . . .

I can: apply what I know about the water cycle to my own geographic area.

FIGURE 3. Self-check: Show Me or Tell Me example.

3. Next, ask students to decide how they will demonstrate that learning. Students can have the option of showing you they have mastered the learning target or telling you information that demonstrates knowledge. When students first begin to self-assess, teachers may need to provide more guidance, but eventually, teachers should expect students to design their own self-assessments.
4. Ask students to complete the Show Me or Tell Me section of the form. The "Show Me" evidence of learning can be a drawing, writing sample, photograph, completed problem, written explanation, or any other appropriate evidence. If the "Tell Me" option is selected, then provide a time and place for the student to provide an oral explanation or demonstration. In some cases, your students may wish to combine the two formats and do some showing and some telling.
5. After you have checked the students' Show Me or Tell Me forms to see if they have satisfactorily demonstrated mastery of the learning target, then they can set their next learning goal.
6. If the self-check was used as a preassessment and the students clearly demonstrated their knowledge of the learning target, then the students should be provided with enrichment activities in lieu of sitting through the whole-class instruction or activities. If not, the students can participate in the planned instruction.

7. Enrichment activities can include independent study, a more in-depth investigation of the topic, or a broader examination of related issues, technical applications, or other options. Ask the student to set a goal and document it.

Students could use the Choose It and Do It strategy (p. 54) and complete contracted work or complete a Challenge Station Planning Form (p. 61) to meet their goal and master their next learning target.

SELF-CHECK: SHOW ME OR TELL ME

Name:____ Date: ________________

As your teacher directs, complete this form to show that you already understand the information about to be taught. Then plan ahead to go further in your learning.

Topic or Objective:____

Learning Target:

I can: ____

____

____

____

____

I will Show You/Tell You. (Check one)

❑ To *show you* I can meet the learning target, here is my evidence (or see attached):

____

____

____

____

____

❑ I will *tell you* what I need to in order to meet the learning target. Please let me know when it is convenient to tell you what I have learned.

My next goal related to this topic or objective is to show or tell you that . . .

I can: ____

____

____

____

____

Ask Two in a Row

Strategy Target

- Assessment

Purpose

Educators who work with advanced learners recognize the importance of questioning. Research has consistently stressed that teachers should ask a high percentage of questions that require higher order thinking, are divergent, and are open ended. Shaunessy (1999) and others have described different types of "thinking" questions, including:

- inference questions,
- interpretation questions,
- questions about hypotheses, and
- reflective questions.

One effective strategy that teachers can use to ensure that they are asking not just knowledge and comprehension questions is to "Ask Two in a Row." (An Ask Two in a Row form with sample questions is provided at the end of the section.) By asking the second, follow-up question, which is a higher level question, teachers require students to think more deeply. When students answer orally, they model their thinking and reasoning for the whole class.

Process

Ask Two in a Row is simple. The following steps explain how this strategy works:

1. When designing lesson plans, whether individually or in a group, teachers should think about what questions they want to ask during instruction. Different parts of a lesson or unit of instruction will require different types of questions.
2. After deciding on the content questions to ask during instruction, review the choices of second questions on the form provided at the end of the section. Decide which

follow-up question makes sense for each original question. (You can always add to the list of second questions.)

3. After asking a student a first question (which may be a lower level knowledge, comprehension, or application question), follow it immediately with the second question. Ask two questions in a row. For example, "What operation did you first use to solve the problem?" could be followed by, "Why did you choose that operation?"
4. Allow students enough time to think and to share the answer to their second question. Make sure other students are listening so they hear the reasoning and thinking behind the second answer.

ASK TWO IN A ROW: SECOND QUESTIONS

2nd Question What evidence do you have to support your answer?	**2nd Question** How did you make that decision?
2nd Question Explain how you reached that conclusion and not another.	**2nd Question** How do you know that?
2nd Question What key elements did you consider before answering that question?	**2nd Question** What inferences can you draw from that?
2nd Question Based on what you just concluded, what do you predict will happen next?	**2nd Question** Were there any clues to help you find that answer?
2nd Question What information would make you change your answer?	**2nd Question** Is there another reasonable answer or explanation?
2nd Question Do you think your answer is correct? If so, why? If not, why not?	**2nd Question** Can you persuade us that you know what you said is correct?
2nd Question Give an example of a similar situation or problem.	**2nd Question** How did you rule out the other possible answers?
2nd Question How does this relate to real life?	**2nd Question** What do you think the next problem or dilemma will be?

Hold That Thought

Strategy Targets

- Instruction
- Assessment

Purpose

Unlike summative assessments, which measure learning at the end of a unit, course, semester, or school year, formative assessments are intended to give teachers information about their students' learning while still teaching the content. When used effectively, formative assessments help teachers make instructional decisions, such as who might need pre- or reteaching, which specific objectives have not been mastered, and who should participate in small-group or individualized instruction.

There are many excellent tools and strategies for quick, easy, and effective formative assessments. However, not all formative assessments address the needs of advanced learners. Hold That Thought is a strategy that is similar to exit cards, which are commonly used to determine student learning after a lesson or activity. Exit cards are a great resource, and many teachers use them to ask students what the key point of the lesson was, whether there was anything they did not understand, and any questions they might have.

Hold That Thought can be thought of as an amped-up exit card designed specifically for use with advanced learners both as they exit class and then again during review the next day. Hold That Thought cards ask higher level questions and raise expectations for students to think about what they have learned. In particular, Sheffield's (2000) work on assessment suggested that teachers' formative assessments should try to determine depth of understanding, fluency, flexibility, originality, elaboration, generalizations, and extensions. The first step, then, is to ask good questions. After students write a response, teachers can refer to students' responses a second time when reviewing. This allows for modeling of higher order thinking for *all* students. Some sample Hold That Thought cards are provided at the end of the section.

HOLD THAT THOUGHT CARDS

What is the relationship between percentages and fractions? These are related by both represent parts of a whole and/or because of percentages can be represented as fractions.

FIGURE 4. Sample Hold That Thought card.

Process

Using Hold That Thought cards is simple (see an example completed card in Figure 4). Just follow these steps:

1. Decide on the higher order thinking questions that are most important and that will indicate students' deep understanding of the content. Use the Hold That Thought cards as prompts and write your questions either on the cards themselves or on blank cards of your own design. Students can also copy assigned questions from a list. The Hold That Thought cards address the constructs mentioned above (depth of understanding, fluency, flexibility, originality, elaboration, generalizations, and extensions) and also include verbs commonly used in high-level questions from Bloom's taxonomy (e.g., analyzing, evaluating, creating).
2. At the end of a lesson or class period, present each student with one Hold That Thought card, as you would an exit slip. You can give the same question to more than one student. You can also add some lower level questions (e.g., remembering, understanding, and applying). The key point in this part of the process is to challenge advanced learners, so make sure that their questions are from the Hold That Thought cards included in this section or are drawn from Bloom's higher levels. (Keep in mind that you can always create your own question/answer formats. We have provided some as quick and easy tools, but we realize the possibilities are endless.)
3. Each student should answer his or her question and put it in a basket or folder before leaving class.
4. Before the next class, review students' responses. After reading through all students' responses, select some Hold That Thought cards that indicate students' deep understanding, flexibility, originality, etc. This step differentiates traditional exit slips from Hold That Thought questions and responses. Typically, teachers check students' exit slips and then make some decisions about reteaching. We suggest that you use Hold That Thought questions and responses as models for creative thinking, problem solving, and making connections.
5. In order to do this, begin instruction the next day by selecting the cards that have questions and responses you want to emphasize. Ask specific students to explain their responses so that all students hear their reasoning. Focus on your advanced learners and their higher order questions and answer. This type of "think aloud" response is good for students who may be struggling but is also helpful for advanced

learners who can be asked to justify their reasoning, refine their responses, get more specific, provide examples, and explain what they were thinking.

6. Allow other students to elaborate, challenge, agree/disagree, and make connections to other learning. This follow-up process makes formative assessment an integral and critical part of instruction.

HOLD THAT THOUGHT CARDS

What is another way to ____?   Another way I might _________________________ is ________________________.
What would you need in order to create __________________________________?   I would need __________________________ to create ________________________.
How would you justify ____?   I would justify _____________________________ by ________________________.
What is the importance of ____?   ___________________ is important/not important because ________________________.
What evidence is there of ____?   __________________________________ is evidence of ________________________.
What can you infer about ______________________________________ and why?   I would infer ___________________________ because ________________________.
How would you prioritize ____?   I would prioritize ____________________________ by ________________________.
What is the relationship between _________________ and ________________________?   These are related by ________________ and/or because of ________________________.
Explain how ______________________________ is like ________________________.   _________________ is like _______________ because ________________________.
What can you conclude about ____? Why?   I can conclude that _______________________ because ________________________.
What evidence is there of ____?   __________________________________ is evidence of ________________________.
How else could you use the same ideas, components, or parts to create something else?   I could use ______________________________ to create ________________________.

I Want to Know

Strategy Targets

- Content
- Instruction

Purpose

Curiosity is a common characteristic of gifted students. Using an I Want to Know card (a sample of which is provided at the end of this section) is a perfect way to encourage curiosity and can be used two ways:

- to allow students who are curious to ask questions, and/or
- to provide advanced learners with an opportunity to satisfy someone else's curiosity through independent research.

Process

This strategy is simple to use if you follow these steps:

1. I Want to Know can be used at almost any time during instruction. Before beginning to implement the strategy, explain it to students, including how to use the I Want to Know cards (see a sample completed card in Figure 5). As long as the cards are accessible and there is a place designated for students to put them after filling them out, no other special steps need to be taken.
2. Throughout a unit or lesson, when a student wants to know more about the topic, ask the student to complete an I Want to Know card and place it in a box, file, or folder. Tell your students to complete a card if what they want to know is beyond the scope of the curriculum or objectives, is highly unusual, or is on a related topic. Reserve the cards for these questions, not for typical questions on the topic that will be discussed or answered in class.

I WANT TO KNOW

Topic/Unit: Organisms and Environment

I want to know how food webs are affected when one or more links in the web are threatened.

I want to know, too, and I will find the answer.

Student
(Name)

Please tell the teacher when you have found the information and would like to share it with the class.

FIGURE 5. Sample I Want To Know card.

3. At appropriate times during the lesson or unit of instruction, read the cards aloud to students. If a student knows the answer, allow him or her to share it with the group.
4. However, if no student knows the answer, allow students to volunteer to find the answer through independent research. Decide if you want to grade this research, provide the student with extra credit points, or keep track of all of the students' independent work as part of a team effort.
5. After a student has found or learned the information that another student wants to know, ask him or her to share with the whole class.
6. Finally, celebrate the curiosity and independence of your students!

I WANT TO KNOW

Topic/Unit: ________________ ________________ I want to know ________________ ________________ ________________ ________________ ________________ ________________ ________________ ________________. I want to know, too, and I will find the answer. ________________ (Name) Please tell the teacher when you have found the information and would like to share it with the class.	Topic/Unit: ________________ ________________ I want to know ________________ ________________ ________________ ________________ ________________ ________________ ________________ ________________. I want to know, too, and I will find the answer. ________________ (Name) Please tell the teacher when you have found the information and would like to share it with the class.
Topic/Unit: ________________ ________________ I want to know ________________ ________________ ________________ ________________ ________________ ________________ ________________ ________________. I want to know, too, and I will find the answer. ________________ (Name) Please tell the teacher when you have found the information and would like to share it with the class.	Topic/Unit: ________________ ________________ I want to know ________________ ________________ ________________ ________________ ________________ ________________ ________________ ________________. I want to know, too, and I will find the answer. ________________ (Name) Please tell the teacher when you have found the information and would like to share it with the class.

Make It Better

Strategy Targets

- Content
- Instruction

Purpose

Teachers of advanced learners should develop patterns of instruction that include asking challenging questions and encouraging high-level thinking. Although some strategies require a lot of planning and may be very involved, others are relatively simple to understand and use. The Make It Better strategy develops the habit of consistently engaging students and requires them to think critically and produce results that go beyond the basics.

Process

Make It Better combines questioning patterns with problem solving. The strategy can be used at any time before, during, or after a lesson. A sample Make It Better chart is provided at the end of the section. Just use the following steps to implement the strategy.

1. Before using the strategy, make sure the lesson is planned completely. Decide when to use Make It Better. It could be a great attention grabber for the beginning of class, a nice way to check understanding during the lesson, and/or an effective way to review.
2. Explain the process to the students before using the Make It Better chart. Make sure they understand by modeling and then having students practice with a concrete example. (For example, "You did a presentation but no one listened. How could you make it better?") Fill in the chart as you explain, model, and practice.
3. When you reach the point in the lesson at which you want to ask students to problem solve, pose the question and allow them to select one or more strategies in the middle column on the chart.
4. After they have considered and applied one or more of the strategies, ask students to explain how they "made it better."

MAKE IT BETTER

Name:____ Date: ____________________

1. As you read, discuss, and learn, your teacher will ask you about how you can change things to make them better. You can use this chart to help you.
2. Describe what needs to change in the first column, then suggest some ways to change it, and then describe how and why you have made your selection better.

Here is the situation, object, or product.	Here are some ways to change it and make it better. (Choose at least one strategy.)	Now explain how you have made it better.
The object is not effective because . . .	◦ Add something. ◦ Delete something. ◦ Change a part/detail. ◦ Flip it forward or backward. ◦ Start over. ◦ Use something a different way. ◦ Make it like something else. ◦ Substitute one thing for another. ◦ Add a visual. ◦ Change the purpose. ◦ Ask a friend.	
The solution to the problem doesn't work because . . .		
This written passage could be better if . . .		
This situation is a problem because . . .		
The design doesn't work and it needs . . .		
The project isn't as good as it could be because . . .		

Here is the situation, object, or product.		Now explain how you have made it better.
The ending of the story could be more interesting if . . .		
This drawing/photograph would be better if . . .		
I could find the answer more easily by . . .		
The argument for/against the issue would be more effective if . . .		
People would understand the debate if . . .		
The resolution to the conflict could be more easily implemented if . . .		

Vocabulary Stretchers

Strategy Targets

- Content
- Instruction

Purpose

Although many students who are gifted and talented have advanced and extensive vocabularies, not all of them do. Students who have very specific interests and are highly gifted in one area may have mastered the vocabulary unique to that discipline but may lack vocabulary skills in other areas. In addition, students' understanding of content can be extensive, but using vocabulary in written assignments or in discussions can still be a challenge. In addition to reading instruction based on high-level critical thinking and vocabulary development through reading, advanced learners can often benefit from vocabulary development activities that stretch and extend their knowledge (Renzulli, 1977).

Because we know that many students do well with visual supports for vocabulary, it is important to expose advanced learners to graphic tools that support them in stretching their thinking and going beyond what they already know. This strategy, Vocabulary Stretchers, focuses on two effective ways to increase students' vocabulary skills: The first tool, Fill in the Blanks, emphasizes opposites, and the second tool, Analogy Frame, uses analogies. Both tools are provided at the end of the section.

Process

To use the first graphic tool, Fill in the Blanks, follow the steps below.

1. Review basic information about opposites and neutral words. Explain how some words' meanings are powerful and extreme, while other words have more neutral, less evocative meanings.

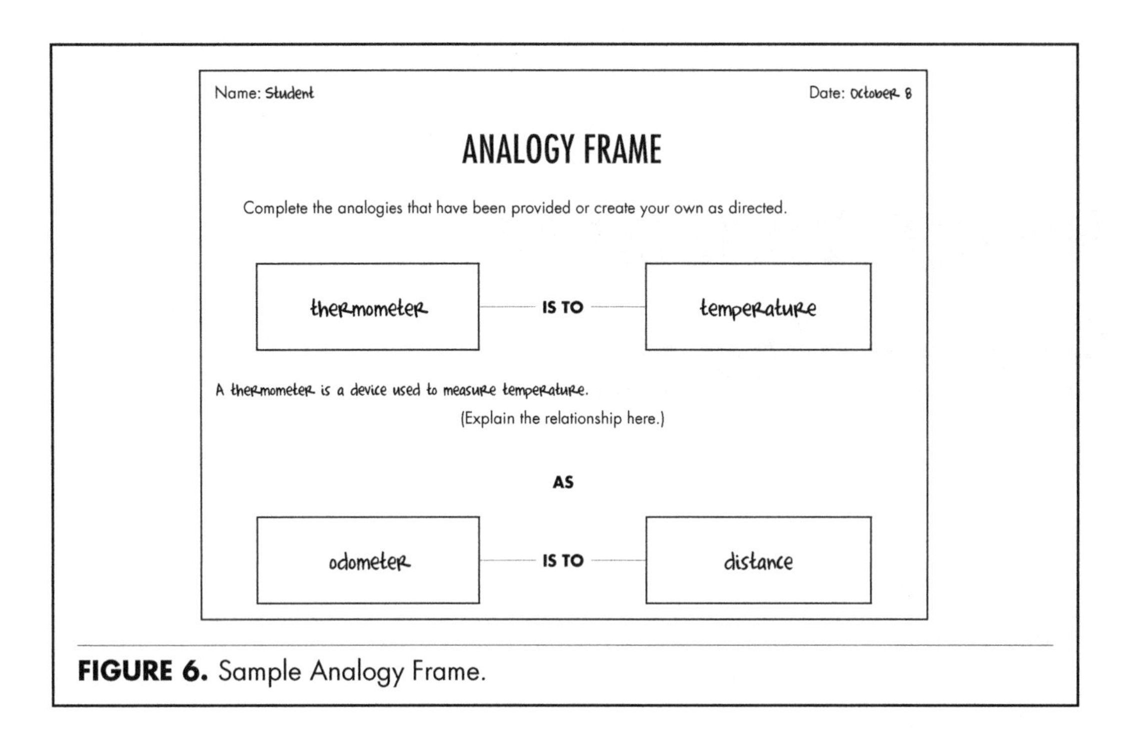

FIGURE 6. Sample Analogy Frame.

2. Share some examples with students. Write the two opposite words in the right- and left-side boxes on one line of the graphic. Explain that words in the middle of the two extremes might be more difficult to generate and defend. Allow students to explain why they chose the words they did when they complete the graphic.

Note that this exercise might be more difficult for adjectives than for nouns or verbs. For example, an animal can be described as ferocious or, at the other extreme, gentle. Other animals in between those two extremes could be described as emotionally stable or variable, but all students might not agree upon those terms. However, if the two opposite words are nouns like *war* and *peace*, there can be many words between the two, including *unrest, stability, uprisings, revolts, civil disobedience*, and others whose meanings are clearly between the two extremes. Teachers can expand the Fill in the Blank forms to include more options but should plan to follow up with a discussion in which students explain and defend their responses.

To use the Analogy Frame, follow the steps below (see a sample completed frame in Figure 6).

1. Explain or review what analogies are (generally described as a comparison based on similarities between like features). If students do not have a lot of experience creating analogies, provide them with examples and give them a lot of guided practice before they complete this activity on their own. Teachers can use the Analogy Frame both for instruction and for students to complete on their own.
2. Introduce the frame with the top half already completed. For example, you could use a simple analogy like *thermometer is to temperature.* Ask students to explain

the relationship, which in this case is, *A thermometer is a device used to measure temperature*. Write a brief summary of the relationship on the middle line.
3. Next, provide students with a word in the first box on the bottom line. For example, the word *odometer* could be used.
4. Review the relationship with students.
5. Finally, ask students to provide the last word, which has the same relationship to odometer as temperature has to thermometer (i.e., distance).
6. When students first use the Analogy Frame, teachers can provide a list of analogies to write in the top half of the graphic and then students can complete them.
7. However, advanced learners can and should create their own analogies and explain to their peers and teachers why they chose the words they did and what the relationships mean.

FILL IN THE BLANKS

Fill in the blanks with words that have meanings related to the two opposite words.

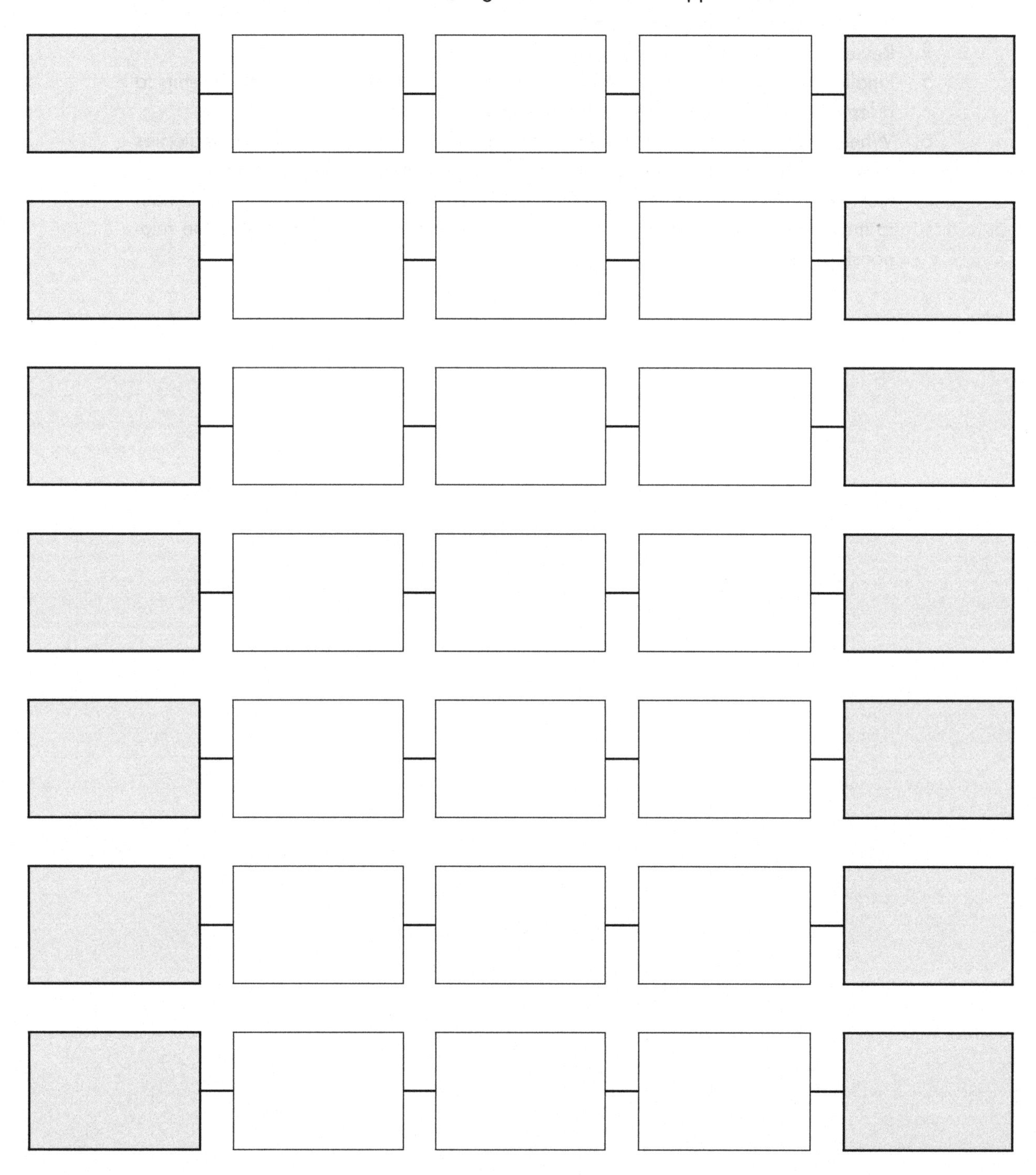

ANALOGY FRAME

Name:____ Date: ________________

Complete the analogies that have been provided or create your own as directed.

IS TO

(Explain the relationship here.)

AS

IS TO

TIPS (Themes, Issues, and Problems)

Strategy Targets

- Content
- Instruction

Purpose

TIPS (themes, issues, and problems) is a strategy that extends the curriculum for advanced learners. Although advanced learners sometimes go deeper into a topic (investigating it in greater detail and becoming "experts"), they can also study a topic more broadly. Expanding the breadth of learning related to a topic allows advanced learners to explore related or similar topics and make connections among them.

Here are some very basic explanations of TIPS, which teachers can discuss with students:

- ***Themes*** relate to subject matter and messages. When students study topics with similar subject matter, they are usually focusing on similar themes.
- ***Issues*** are topics for debate and discussion. Usually, people agree or disagree on some issues as being important, which is why they will discuss them.
- ***Problems*** are often difficult situations and require solutions or in some way need to be dealt with.

Exploring TIPS related to a topic or concept that students are already studying often happens naturally. However, for advanced learners who likely already know basic information, exploring TIPS can extend the curriculum in meaningful and interesting ways. In this strategy, students first generate TIPS that are related to the topic or concept they are studying.

Process

The TIPS strategy requires some teaching and practice, but students and teachers should begin to feel comfortable with it if they follow these steps (see an example in Figure 7):

THEMES

We are studying the relationship between supply and demand in economics.

Related themes are:

- Basic principles of economics may hold true over time but seem inaccurate in the short term.
- The price of a product results from negotiation between the buyer and the seller.
- The amount and diversity of production affects equilibrium.

FIGURE 7. Sample TIPS strategy.

1. TIPS can be used during almost any unit of instruction. First, make sure everyone is clear on the key concept(s) of the unit (i.e., what students should "understand"). For example, "Students will understand the relationship between supply and demand in economics."
2. After articulating what students should understand, teachers can begin to plan extended learning activities for advanced learners by identifying related TIPS: themes, issues, or problems. Students can also suggest their own TIPS.
3. To get students started, use the TIPS forms provided and teach your students (in groups of three to five) a simple brainstorming technique. You can easily create similar TIPS sheets yourself. When the TIPS brainstorming forms are ready, give students directions like these:
   - "You are going to generate ideas for themes, issues, or problems that are related to the key concept we are studying."
   - "First, discuss the concept with your partner or group. Take 2 minutes each to explain what you think the concept is and how well you understand it."
   - "Next, look at the three brainstorming forms on the table. You will see that each page includes the concept as well as one of these three words: themes, issues, or problems."
   - "You will have 5 minutes to think of as many related themes, issues, or problems as you can."
   - "Choose any of the forms you like and quickly write a word or phrase that explains your idea. Then return the form to the center of the table."
   - "You may write as many ideas as you like on any of the forms, so you may contribute no ideas to themes, but five ideas to problems. "
   - "Keep writing and moving the papers back and forth from the center of the table until directed to stop."
   - "Reading others' ideas is fine if you can do so quickly. This may prompt another idea."
   - "Do not talk during the process because your talking may unduly influence another student and dissuade him or her from proposing an idea."

4. After students have finished brainstorming, ask them to share and discuss the themes, issues, and problems related to the key concept(s) in the current unit of instruction. For example, the supply and demand concept could have:

- ***Themes*** that include ways in which basic principles of economics may hold true over time but seem inaccurate in the short term,
- ***Issues*** like the way politics can disrupt typical supply and demand patterns, and
- ***Problems*** like how to deal with shortages in ways that are socially responsible.

5. Follow up with a discussion. Make sure your students have identified meaningful TIPS and that they are fully engaged in the process. Help them narrow their interests.
6. Finally, assign specific students, partners, or small groups to a theme, issue, or problem. To investigate the assigned TIP, students can do a WebQuest, use the next strategy in this book (TIPS: Independent Study), which provides an independent study guide, or follow another agreed-upon structure.

THEMES

We are studying ____.

Related themes are:

ISSUES

We are studying ______________________________.

Related themes are:

PROBLEMS

We are studying ____.

Related themes are:

TIPS
Independent Study

Strategy Targets

- Content
- Instruction

Purpose

The previous strategy, TIPS (Themes, Issues, and Problems), provided a format and a process to help students extend their study of the curriculum by generating themes, issues, and problems that relate to the topic or concept being studied in class but are broader in scope.

This related strategy provides teachers with tools that can be used for independent study of one or more of the TIPS they and students decide to investigate. Independent studies not only allow students to deepen or broaden their knowledge, they also allow students to move at an individualized pace, which should keep them engaged and interested. However, even advanced learners usually need some structure as they work independently.

Process

To structure independent study of a TIP, follow these steps:

1. Use the Weekly Planning Guide, provided at the end of this section, to identify the TIP the student or group has chosen to investigate further. Work with students to complete the planning guide so that there are goals and activities, as well as resources identified for each day. Remember that resources can include a wide variety of options like interviews; websites and other online resources; visual media; and print material like books, newspapers, and magazines.
2. Encourage students to be creative and to have a method of presentation in mind as they complete their independent study. Students and teachers should both initial the form to indicate agreement and understanding of the goals, activities, and resources.

3. At the end of each day, student(s) should evaluate their progress individually and then in a discussion with the teacher. Teachers should ask questions about both the process and the product, including what was studied and what was completed. Students should share evidence of completion. Both students and teachers can initial the Progress and Product Form (also provided at the end of this section) each day if all activities and goals have been completed.
4. Finally, each student who completes an independent study should present what they learned to their peers, other students in the school, and/or adults. The type of presentation should be mutually agreed upon between the teacher and the student. A rubric or checklist can be used for evaluation of the final presentation and any other products created during the independent study.

WEEKLY PLANNING GUIDE

Name:____ Date: ________________

What is the topic or concept?

What is your TIP?

What question(s) do you have about your TIP?

Daily Goals/Activities	Resources	Initials
Monday		
Tuesday		
Wednesday		
Thursday		
Friday		

PROGRESS AND PRODUCT FORM

Name:____ Date: ________________

What is the topic or concept?
What is your TIP?
What question(s) did you answer about your TIP?

Daily Goals/Activities	What did you accomplish?	Initials
Monday	I studied ________________________ . I completed ________________________ .	
Tuesday	I studied ________________________ . I completed ________________________ .	
Wednesday	I studied ________________________ . I completed ________________________ .	
Thursday	I studied ________________________ . I completed ________________________ .	
Friday	I studied ________________________ . I completed ________________________ .	

Method of presentation: ____

(e.g., oral report, demonstration, display, electronic display, etc.)

That's Interesting

Strategy Target

- Content

Purpose

Unfortunately, some students are advanced learners but still do not achieve well academically. There are many reasons that students underachieve. One possible reason for student underachievement is a lack of motivation. When a student, whether an advanced learner or not, is bored with the curriculum and not motivated to actively engage in learning, they may not do well regardless of how gifted and talented they might be.

Advanced learners often have specific and specialized interests. Because many of their interests differ from their peers, differentiating the curriculum is important. Other strategies in this book offer suggestions for how to structure contracts, independent study, and challenging learning stations. All of these and other related ideas can be effective for advanced learners.

The content addressed in these and other instructional arrangements can be based, at least in part, on a student's individual interests. All teachers are expected to address national, state, and local standards and curricula. However, within the required goals and objectives, it is often possible to allow advanced learners to pursue topics of special interest to them, especially when those topics can be woven into the overall curriculum framework. That's Interesting is a strategy to help teachers and students identify the students' interests and then extend or enrich the curriculum based on those interests. A That's Interesting card is provided at the end of the section.

Process

To help with planning that integrates students' special interests into instruction, consider these steps:

1. Set aside time to have a private discussion with the student. It is not necessary to have a formal interview time. Sharing lunch or meeting during an advisory or intervention class period will usually provide enough time, and less formality might facilitate open sharing of information.
2. After the student has discussed some of his or her special interests, narrow the list to three or four topics. If the student is so limited that he or she can identify only one special interest, continue the discussion and suggest other topics that might be of interest.
3. In the process of planning instruction, decide if the student's special interest(s) matches the topic or content being taught.
4. Then decide if extension or enrichment (or both) would be the most effective way to encourage student learning. Although these two terms are often used interchangeably, teachers who work and plan together can agree on what they mean by each term. Often, *enrichment* is used to describe learning that goes beyond the general curriculum, and *extension* usually refers to the extension of learning to other content areas or topics.
5. After determining which of the student's special interests will be part of the content, the mode of study can be determined. There are many ideas in this book for contracts, independent study, learning stations or centers, or others. Advanced learners can often go well beyond anything their teachers expect when concentrating on something they enjoy and find interesting.

THAT'S INTERESTING

Name: ______________________________ Date: ____________

Student's special interests include: ______________________________

____

____

____

____

This week's topic/goal/objective is: ______________________________

To ***enrich*** the content, the assignment will be: ______________________________

____

____

____

____

THAT'S INTERESTING

Name: ______________________________ Date: ____________

Student's special interests include: ______________________________

____

____

____

____

This week's topic/goal/objective is: ______________________________

To ***enrich*** the content, the assignment will be: ______________________________

____

____

____

____

Choose It and Do It

Strategy Target

- Content

Purpose

Learning contracts can be written for any curriculum area and can enrich students' learning beyond the basic curriculum while also providing challenge. Contracts are especially useful in classrooms in which cluster grouping of advanced learners is used because they allow students to work at a pace appropriate for their knowledge and skill level.

The Choose It and Do It strategy is a learning contract that can be used with advanced learners and other students who sometimes are best served by working independently. A Choose It and Do It contract is provided at the end of this section (see a sample completed contract in Figure 8). Choose It and Do It is intended for short-term use. The format of the contract allows teachers to mandate some assignments but also give students choices about other learning tasks. Students are asked to self-evaluate while teachers also provide feedback.

Process

To use the Choose It and Do It strategy, follow these steps:

1. After identifying the learning objective that will be addressed, teachers should decide on one to three Must Do (required) tasks and one to three May Do (optional) tasks.
2. Explain to the students how many of each type of task they must complete. If any of the tasks require a rubric for assessment, indicate that at the bottom of the form and attach the rubric to the contract. (This is recommended if products are to be created.)
3. Discuss the tasks and the due dates with the students and write them on the form. Again, Choose It and Do It is intended for short-term use, so a 1–5-day timeline is appropriate.

CHOOSE IT AND DO IT

Name: Hannah H.		Date: 3/5-3/12
Teacher: Ms. Conley		
Course/Subject: Science		
Objective(s): Describe forces and energy transformations in everyday situations		
***Must Do* Tasks: Complete 3**	***May Do* Tasks: Complete 2**	**Dates Due**
1. Do vocabulary match. 2. Construct a simple electromagnet. 3. Identify complete v. incomplete circuits.	1. Construct a simple electric motor and explain how it works. 2. Create a flow diagram explaining how current flows. 3. Design an experiment with static electricity showing how particles affect each other.	Must Do: March 5 May Do: March 12

Student Self-Evaluation:

Did I use my time effectively? (Yes)/No

Did I complete all tasks? (Yes)/No

What could I do differently? Gather materials ahead of time.

The best thing about this contract was I had choices.

One thing I would change about this contract is I would like to work with someone.

Teacher Evaluation:

Student completed all tasks. (Yes)/No

Student used time effectively. (Yes)/No

Student was organized and prepared. Yes/(No)

Student followed class and contract rules. (Yes)/No

Comments: Materials organization and preparation were issues. We will work at this together.

Will a rubric be used for assessment? (Yes)/No -For the experiment.
If so, please attach.

FIGURE 8. Sample Choose It and Do It contract.

4. Before the students begin to work on the contract tasks, discuss and clarify the following:
   - what resources can and should be used;
   - what guidelines are in place for the use of electronics, like computers or tablets;
   - rules for appropriate behavior;
   - how all assignments will be evaluated, including any rubrics, as mentioned above; and
   - whether the students may complete some tasks with a partner or small group rather than individually.

5. Teachers should check in regularly with students who are using even short-term learning contracts to ensure that they are making good use of their time and that they are clear about what is expected.

6. After the contract time period has ended, the students and teacher should complete the evaluations on the form, and then the teacher should assign grades to the students' work.
7. If a student has problems working independently the first time or two a contract is used, do not give up. Some students need more structure and support than others but gradually adjust and become more self-directed.

CHOOSE IT AND DO IT

<table>
<tr><td colspan="2">Name:</td><td colspan="2">Date:</td></tr>
<tr><td colspan="4">Teacher:</td></tr>
<tr><td colspan="4">Course/Subject:</td></tr>
<tr><td colspan="4">Objective(s):</td></tr>
<tr><td>Must Do Tasks: Complete ______</td><td colspan="2">May Do Tasks: Complete ______</td><td>Dates Due</td></tr>
<tr><td>1. ______________________
2. ______________________
3. ______________________</td><td colspan="2">1. ______________________
2. ______________________
3. ______________________</td><td></td></tr>
</table>

Student Self-Evaluation:

Did I use my time effectively? Yes/No

Did I complete all tasks? Yes/No

What could I do differently? ____

The best thing about this contract was ______________________________________

One thing I would change about this contract is ______________________________

Teacher Evaluation:

Student completed all tasks. Yes/No

Student used time effectively. Yes/No

Student was organized and prepared. Yes/No

Student followed class and contract rules. Yes/No

Comments: ____

____

____

Will a rubric be used for assessment? Yes/No
If so, please attach.

Strategic Choices

Strategy Targets

- Content
- Instruction

Purpose

Professional development, books and materials, and school district guidelines have encouraged teachers to differentiate to meet the needs of individual students in their classrooms. Often, teachers use tiered objectives, menus, and choices to accomplish this differentiation.

Providing students with choices not only allows for a systematic way of changing the level of knowledge required to demonstrate learning, the process is often motivating for students because they have some control over their own learning. The nature of the task, the level of challenge, and the type of activity can all be designed with a variety of learners in mind.

For advanced learners, providing choices that require higher order thinking, independent learning, and demonstration of mastery through demonstration or production makes the process exciting and effective. The Strategic Choices form provided at the end of this section gives teachers a template so that they can quickly and easily create a choice form for long-term and/or recurring assignments. We suggest that users create an electronic file with the choice template so that it can be used to create the choice options without the need to redesign a new form each time new choices are provided.

Process

To use the Strategic Choices strategy, follow this process:

1. When planning instruction, review the goals and objectives. Because this strategy is focused on long-term or recurring assignments, be sure to teach students early in the year how to complete the assignments each week or each marking period.
2. Next, design the learning activities. Note that the form, entitled Long-Term Planning for Strategic Choices, is for teacher planning. Teachers can decide whether to tell students what level of learning they are working on, but all learners should be encouraged to challenge themselves with higher order thinking.
3. This form is useful for long units of instruction, but also for instruction that is repeated throughout the school year. For example, in English/language arts, students often have writing, grammar, or reading assignments each week or marking period. Planning various levels of assignments for 3 to 6 weeks may take a little more time in the beginning but is very efficient over the course of time. Simply indicate whether a specific assignment was selected by the student and approved by the teacher and write the due date.
4. When explaining each choice, make sure that advanced learners are clear about your expectations for them. Also inform parents that their child's instruction will be differentiated.
5. At the appropriate time in the instructional sequence, allow students to choose assignments and complete them within a clear timeline. Decide ahead of time how to evaluate products, whether with rubrics, checklists, or rating scales.

LONG-TERM PLANNING FOR STRATEGIC CHOICES

Assignment 1	Assignment 2	Assignment 3
Knowledge Name: ____________ Choice? Yes/No Approved? Yes/No Date Due: ____________	Knowledge Name: ____________ Choice? Yes/No Approved? Yes/No Date Due: ____________	Knowledge Name: ____________ Choice? Yes/No Approved? Yes/No Date Due: ____________
Comprehension Name: ____________ Choice? Yes/No Approved? Yes/No Date Due: ____________	Comprehension Name: ____________ Choice? Yes/No Approved? Yes/No Date Due: ____________	Comprehension Name: ____________ Choice? Yes/No Approved? Yes/No Date Due: ____________
Application Name: ____________ Choice? Yes/No Approved? Yes/No Date Due: ____________	Application Name: ____________ Choice? Yes/No Approved? Yes/No Date Due: ____________	Application Name: ____________ Choice? Yes/No Approved? Yes/No Date Due: ____________
Analysis Name: ____________ Choice? Yes/No Approved? Yes/No Date Due: ____________	Analysis Name: ____________ Choice? Yes/No Approved? Yes/No Date Due: ____________	Analysis Name: ____________ Choice? Yes/No Approved? Yes/No Date Due: ____________
Synthesis Name: ____________ Choice? Yes/No Approved? Yes/No Date Due: ____________	Synthesis Name: ____________ Choice? Yes/No Approved? Yes/No Date Due: ____________	Synthesis Name: ____________ Choice? Yes/No Approved? Yes/No Date Due: ____________
Evaluation Name: ____________ Choice? Yes/No Approved? Yes/No Date Due: ____________	Evaluation Name: ____________ Choice? Yes/No Approved? Yes/No Date Due: ____________	Evaluation Name: ____________ Choice? Yes/No Approved? Yes/No Date Due: ____________

Challenge Stations

Strategy Targets

- Instruction
- Content

Purpose

We have discussed elsewhere in this book ways in which Bloom's taxonomy can be used to help teachers formulate higher order thinking activities. Teachers of advanced learners should also be aware of another construct that is sometimes referred to when planning learning activities: Webb's Depth of Knowledge.

Webb's Depth of Knowledge (DOK) was originally designed as a process and criteria for aligning standards and standardized curricula. Tasks that students are expected to complete are categorized based on the cognitive expectation, or depth of knowledge, required. Webb's DOK levels include: (1) Recall and Reproduction, (2) Skills and Concepts, (3) Short-Term Strategic Thinking, and (4) Extended Thinking. Explanations of Webb's levels emphasize that a task's DOK level is *not* totally dependent on the verb used to describe the task, nor is it all about the level of difficulty. It is the complexity of a learning task that matters (Mississippi State University, 2009).

Learning stations and centers are often used to provide practice opportunities for students after direct instruction. Stations can include a variety of activities that students complete as they rotate through them. Learning stations are typically designed to focus on specific skills, activities, and interests. Unfortunately, learning stations, like all other instructional arrangements, can lack rigor and may not be engaging for students. It is important that learning stations for advanced learners be challenging and engaging, and they should achieve the goal of extending students' learning. This strategy, Challenge Stations, provides a tool for planning learning stations with Webb's Depth of Knowledge levels in mind. When used as guide during the lesson planning process, it can help ensure that stations meet the needs of advanced learners who may not need much practice but certainly do need engaging and challenging tasks.

Process

To use the Challenge Stations strategy, use the Challenge Station Planning Form provided at the end of this section and follow these steps:

1. Because most schools now do common lesson planning, review the Challenge Station Planning Form with your grade level or content area team. After targeting a specific instructional objective, decide how you (and your team) will introduce the content and provide basic instruction to students. Check all of the methods that apply.
2. Next, plan the learning station activities. For your advanced learners, this will usually mean designing tasks that are at the two highest DOK levels, short-term and extended thinking. We have provided a list of products and activities at the end of the section that should help with this process and prompt additional ideas.
3. For each activity, also decide on the materials needed, exactly what students are supposed to do, and how you will check for understanding. Decide if you think each station is a challenge station for advanced learners only or if it can be used for all students.
4. By maintaining a focus on challenge activities during the planning process, teachers can emphasize higher level tasks that are not just rote practice but engaging activities that are complex and that require deep knowledge.
5. At the end of each week or each marking period, review all of the Challenge Station Planning Forms. Decide if you have designed learning stations that will meet the needs of your advanced learners. If you don't see a lot of circles around the "Yes" on the planning form, your team may need to revisit the curriculum and Webb's Depth of Knowledge levels.

CHALLENGE STATION PLANNING FORM

<table>
<tr><td colspan="4">Course/Subject:</td></tr>
<tr><td colspan="4">Objective(s):</td></tr>
<tr><td>Description of Station Instruction</td><td colspan="3">❏ Explanation:
❏ Demonstration:
❏ Teacher/Student Modeling:
❏ Reading Material:
❏ Media:
❏ Vocabulary Instruction:
❏ Other:</td></tr>
<tr><th>Name of Learning Station</th><th>Depth of Knowledge Level</th><th>Materials in Station</th><th>Description of Station</th></tr>
<tr><td>1</td><td>❏ Recall/Reproduction
❏ Skills/Concepts
❏ Short-Term Strategic Thinking
❏ Extended Thinking</td><td>❏ Print:
❏ Technology:
❏ Manipulatives:
❏ Media:
❏ Other:</td><td>Challenge Station? Yes/No
Exactly what will students do?
What is the product, if any?
How will you check for understanding?</td></tr>
<tr><td>2</td><td>❏ Recall/Reproduction
❏ Skills/Concepts
❏ Short-Term Strategic Thinking
❏ Extended Thinking</td><td>❏ Print:
❏ Technology:
❏ Manipulatives:
❏ Media:
❏ Other:</td><td>Challenge Station? Yes/No
Exactly what will students do?
What is the product, if any?
How will you check for understanding?</td></tr>
</table>

Challenge Station Planning Form, continued

Name of Learning Station	Depth of Knowledge Level	Materials in Station	Description of Station
3	❏ Recall/Reproduction ❏ Skills/Concepts ❏ Short-Term Strategic Thinking ❏ Extended Thinking	❏ Print: ❏ Technology: ❏ Manipulatives: ❏ Media: ❏ Other:	Challenge Station? Yes/No Exactly what will students do? What is the product, if any? How will you check for understanding?
4	❏ Recall/Reproduction ❏ Skills/Concepts ❏ Short-Term Strategic Thinking ❏ Extended Thinking	❏ Print: ❏ Technology: ❏ Manipulatives: ❏ Media: ❏ Other:	Challenge Station? Yes/No Exactly what will students do? What is the product, if any? How will you check for understanding?
5	❏ Recall/Reproduction ❏ Skills/Concepts ❏ Short-Term Strategic Thinking ❏ Extended Thinking	❏ Print: ❏ Technology: ❏ Manipulatives: ❏ Media: ❏ Other:	Challenge Station? Yes/No Exactly what will students do? What is the product, if any? How will you check for understanding?

Name of Learning Station	Depth of Knowledge Level	Materials in Station	Description of Station
6	❑ Recall/Reproduction ❑ Skills/Concepts ❑ Short-Term Strategic Thinking ❑ Extended Thinking	❑ Print: ❑ Technology: ❑ Manipulatives: ❑ Media: ❑ Other:	Challenge Station? Yes/No Exactly what will students do? What is the product, if any? How will you check for understanding?

EXAMPLES OF CHALLENGE STATION ACTIVITIES: SHORT-TERM AND EXTENDED STRATEGIC THINKING

Below are examples of Level 3 and 4 activities in Webb's Depth of Knowledge system. Some examples are adapted from Mississippi State University's 2009 publication, *Webb's Depth of Knowledge Guide*.

Possible Products:

- Report
- Program
- Podcast
- Webinar
- Spreadsheet
- Graph
- Outline Chart
- Plan
- Game
- Song
- Website
- Animation
- Video

Possible Activities:

Students will . . .

- Design a questionnaire
- Devise unique and original solutions to problems
- Design a product and a marketing plan for it
- Make a graphic organizer and/or flow chart to explain a process
- Form a panel and conduct a panel discussion
- Write an original song or jingle
- Create tables, graphs, and charts from researched information
- Write a letter or blog post advocating for a cause
- Write a letter to an editor or an editorial that includes specific evidence in support of a position
- Design a menu that includes specific criteria such as calorie and nutrition counts and cost per serving
- Prepare a simulated legal case related to a relevant social issue
- Create a rubric to evaluate an assignment

Problem Solve in Steps

Strategy Targets

- Instruction
- Content

Purpose

There are many problem-solving models that can be used in education as well as other organizations or situations. Teaching students to solve problems not only helps students learn, but the process can be very enjoyable for students. After students who are advanced learners master the process, they can problem solve on their own to complete independent assignments.

Drapeau (2014) suggests a three-step process in which students identify what they don't know, what they think they know, and what they definitely know. This is similar to a traditional K-W-L model (what I already know, what I want to know, and what I learned). Then, students work together to set criteria for solutions. Another option is to brainstorm and prioritize problems, then set criteria and develop a solution. Yet another strategy is to focus on a problem that is agreed upon as the most important problem related to a specific topic and then brainstorm solutions based on agreed-upon characteristics.

However, for advanced learners who have the ability to learn a process and then use it independently, it is helpful to give students a simple step-by-step format, allow them to practice and master the steps, and then let them work on their own. Problem solving assignments can be used throughout the school year to deepen students' learning about topics they are studying and those they find especially interesting.

Process

To use the Problem Solve in Steps strategy, use the forms provided at the end of this section and follow this process:

1. Assign students to groups with three to five students. Assign them either a letter (e.g., Group A, Group B, Group C) or a name (e.g., The Explorers, The Adventurers, The Inventors, The Innovators). It is usually best to have no more than three or four students in each group because decision making may get difficult with larger groups. This process should also work well with partners.
2. The students will be completing three steps to solve a problem:
   - problem finding,
   - solution finding, and
   - writing an action plan.

3. After students have been assigned to their groups, model and provide practice for the problem-solving process. When teaching a problem-solving model for the first time, pick a simple, everyday problem for students to solve. After students are comfortable with the process, begin to use it for problems related to the topics they are studying.
4. Students should first find a problem they want to solve. Using the Problem Finding form, they can identify three potential problems, discuss what is known about each, discuss what needs to be learned about each, and then vote to select one. An easy way to vote is to have each group member assign points: Three points for the problem they think is most important, two points for the next most important problem, and then one point for the problem they do not think is critical. The problem with the highest total number of points is the one to solve.
5. The next step is to find solutions. Using the Solution Finding form provided, teach students to articulate at least three solutions for the problem. Then, they should list the advantages and disadvantages of each solution. Provide some guidance with this step by clarifying whether specific criteria matter. For example, cost may not be a consideration, so even very expensive solutions to the problem can be an option. On the other hand, teachers may want to limit students to solutions that are within a budget. Some criteria teachers may require for consideration can relate to:
   - cost,
   - length of time for implementation,
   - resources involved,
   - personnel required,
   - involvement of specific stakeholders,
   - timelines, or
   - technology support.

   Students should choose at least one solution for implementation. Voting is an option in this part of the process as well.

6. Have students write the solution implementation action plan on the Action Plan: Solution Implementation form. They should consider which materials and methods are necessary to implement the solution(s) selected. Students should also designate specific individuals for implementing the solution.

7. Finally, as part of the problem solving assignment, each group of students should share their problem, solution, and action plan with others. Decisions about timelines and formats for sharing can be made with teacher guidance. Keeping the action plan simple should help students as they formulate practical solutions for challenging problems.
8. When students are proficient in the problem solving process, begin to assign them individual, partner, or small-group problems that they can find solutions for while working independently.

PROBLEM FINDING

Topic: ____________________

Group Members: ____________________ ____________________

____________________ ____________________

Potential Problems	What We Know About the Problem	What We Need to Learn About the Problem	Point Value	Selected?
1				Yes/No
2				Yes/No
3				Yes/No

SOLUTION FINDING

Topic: ______________________________

Group Members: ______________________ ______________________

______________________ ______________________

Problem				
Solutions	**Advantages**	**Disadvantages**	**Point Value**	**Selected?**
1				Yes/No
2				Yes/No
3				Yes/No

ACTION PLAN: SOLUTION IMPLEMENTATION

Topic: ______________________________

Group Members: ______________________ ______________________

______________________ ______________________

Solution	
Materials	
Methods	
Persons Responsible	

Format for Sharing Results of the Problem Solve in Steps Process:

____

____

____

____

Due Date: ______________________

Online Research

Strategy Targets

- Instruction
- Content

Purpose

In classrooms today, students will likely use technology, especially online resources for most of their independent research. Students have grown up with technology and many of them are confident and proficient in their use of smartphones, tablets, and computers. Online, web-based research strategies for advanced learners have been used successfully for several years.

When teachers assign a research project, especially independent research, students may have no problems with the *online* aspect of their assignments because they can navigate the Internet easily. However, students may not know how to meet the *research* expectations. Advanced learners should be taught the basic steps of well-designed, thorough, and cohesive research projects. After teachers are sure they know the process, advanced learners can easily pursue their research and produce amazing reports, presentations, action plans, descriptions, and designs.

Teachers should be prepared to teach basic research skills to students, including:

- how to write research questions;
- how to plan the research project;
- how to gather information, evaluate it, and then eliminate and/or gather more information;
- how to respect others' property and copyrights; and
- how to create a final product to share their research.

Process

Because this strategy is focused on online research, we have gathered a group of online resources that we will describe. Teachers can easily access these websites through the links provided. Many of the sources will also link to other helpful information. We have located the resources, reviewed them, and provided a description in order to help teachers whose time is limited.

In addition, we have provided a Research Plan and a Research Timeline at the end of this section that should help teachers and students as they plan their research. The Research Plan should be completed by the students before beginning their research, as should the timeline. Teachers should approve both the plan and the timelines before beginning. After advanced learners have completed online research with teacher supervision, teachers can expect them to do additional research independently.

Below are some resources to help guide students through online research.

The Buck Institute for Education: http://bie.org/

There are numerous resources on The Buck Institute for Education website, and many of the planning forms are interactive. We strongly recommend this site for educators who are interested in using project-based learning for research. Many schools have taken a project-based learning approach to most of their instruction, with good results for students. Students work to answer a driving question and use research skills and Internet resources. The planning forms on the website include an Essential Elements Checklist (Buck Institute for Education, 2014) that indicates the actions necessary to complete a good research project, including:

- focusing on significant content,
- developing 21st-century competencies,
- engaging students in in-depth inquiry,
- organizing tasks around a driving question,
- establishing a "need to know",
- encouraging voice and choice,
- incorporating critique and revision, and
- including a public audience.

"15 Lesson Plans for Making Students Better Researchers" by Jeff Dunn (2012): http://www.edudemic.com/students-better-online-researchers/

This article includes a lesson plan map linked to Common Core State Standards that has information for teachers who are working with beginner, intermediate, and advanced students as they learn how to conduct effective searches. The information guides students to identify search terms, create inquiries, and understand what deep web resources are. The lesson plans also address how to evaluate search results, how to know which sources to use and which are credible, and how to narrow searches to get the best results. There are specific lesson plans provided for each level of student researcher.

"Doing Internet Research at the Elementary Level" by Mary Beth Hertz (2012): http://www.edutopia.org/blog/elementary-research-mary-beth-hertz

This article discusses Internet research for elementary students. It is a personal account from a teacher, who provides a graphic of the research process she teaches, including:

- what is research?;
- topics, keywords, and search terms;
- testing search terms;
- copyright/plagiarism;
- evaluating sites;
- taking notes/gathering information;
- citation; and
- synthesizing information and sharing results.

The author also provides links to several resources, including EasyBib, which helps students organize their links and has some free educator resources.

"The 6 Online Research Skills Your Students Need" by Hannah Trierweiler Hudson (2014): http://www.scholastic.com/teachers/article/6-online-research-skills-your-students-need

This article was written for educators working with students in grades 6–8. Hudson's key points for students include:

- check your sources,
- ask good questions,
- go beyond the surface,
- be patient,
- respect ownership, and
- use your networks.

The author describes the skills and challenges involved in each of these and provides additional links to resources.

RESEARCH PLAN

Name: ______________________________ Date: ______________

Complete this form and provide it to your teacher for review.

1. I will study this topic: ______________________________

2. My major questions are: ______________________________

3. Other possible questions are: ______________________________

4. Primary search terms are: ______________________________

RESEARCH TIMELINE

Name:____ Date: ______________

Complete this form and provide it to your teacher for review.

Step	Due Date
1. Select the topic.	____________
2. Develop questions.	____________
3. Decide on initial search terms.	____________
4. Locate primary resources.	____________
5. Conduct the research.	____________
6. Locate additional resources, if needed.	____________
7. Complete citations and ensure copyright adherence.	____________
8. Create product.	____________
9. Plan for and present product.	____________

Notes: ____

What's Next?

Strategy Targets

- Instruction
- Content

Purpose

Teachers often provide students with options for what to do when they have finished an assignment and other students are still working. In fact, many classrooms have charts posted that tell students what to do when they are finished.

For advanced learners, "early finishing" occurs often and teachers, especially those in mixed-ability classrooms, will want to plan ahead. Advanced learners will need to have assignments that are not just intended to keep them busy, but are also designed to go beyond the standard grade-level curriculum.

Process

These steps will guide the implementation of What's Next?:

1. First, plan the unit of instruction based on your standards, goals, and objectives.
2. As you plan, especially in team planning, discuss what activities will benefit advanced learners who may already know the basic information. These students are likely to finish any group assignments early and will need to be provided with ability-appropriate assignments and activities.
3. Post the What's Next? choices or provide them on a card for students to complete. A sample What's Next? card is provided at the end of this section (see a completed example in Figure 9).
4. Make sure that the student understands the criteria for completion and grading as well as the due dates for all assignments.

WHAT'S NEXT?

If you have finished your assignment related to: center of a distribution, choose from the menu below. Your teacher will explain when the assignment is due and what the criteria for completion are.

<table>
<tr>
<td>Research ____________________</td>
<td>Study measures of center in greater detail/depth.
1. Change two data points that will change the median but not the mean.
2. Draw two histograms, one with the original data and one with the modified data from #1.
3. Describe when the median would be a better measure than the mean of the center of the distribution.</td>
</tr>
<tr>
<td>Expand to this topic: ____________________</td>
<td>Read print or online information.</td>
</tr>
</table>

FIGURE 9. Sample completed What's Next? card.

WHAT'S NEXT?

If you have finished your assignment related to: ______________________________, choose from the menu below. Your teacher will explain when the assignment is due and what the criteria for completion are.

Research ______________________________	**Study** __________ **in greater detail/depth.**
Expand to this topic: __________________	**Read print or online information**.

ID
Imagine + Do

Strategy Target

- Instruction

Purpose

Sometimes, educators tend to think that creativity is static (i.e., that students either are or are not creative). However, there is evidence that creativity can be encouraged and even taught (Scott, Lertiz, & Mumford, 2004). Teachers should be familiar with some basic models of creativity and recognize that there are several factors that help students be more creative, including knowledge or expertise, thinking skills, and interest or motivation.

In the classroom, the process of stimulating creative thoughts and actions can be interesting and fun when assignments and activities are structured to allow students to be creative. The ID: Imagine + Do strategy is a simple way to design assignments that stimulate students' creative thinking. As you design the choices on the ID Board provided at the end of this section, choose verbs for the assignments that require higher level thinking.

Process

To use the ID: Imagine + Do strategy, follow these steps and use the form provided.

1. For teachers, the first step is to complete both the "imagine" verb phrases and the "do" phrases on the ID Board. For example, for a math unit on shapes, one of the "imagine" verb phrases could be, "Imagine you are a circle and your friend is a sphere." A choice for the "do" activity might be, "Explain the difference between the two of you." (Very advanced learners could be allowed to complete the "imagine" verb phrases on their own before selecting or designing a "do" activity.)
2. Next, explain each option to the students. It might help to insert the word "and" or "then" between the "imagine" verb and the "do" activity. (e.g., "*Pretend* you

are a member of Congress **and** *create* a chart explaining your position on farm subsidies.")

3. If there are specific requirements for the activities/assignments, clarify them. Also set a deadline for completion.
4. Students can then choose any "imagine" verb phrase from the first column and any of the "do" phrases from the second column. Guide the more advanced learners to the more challenging activities.
5. This board can be integrated into an interactive whiteboard and the choices could also be part of a slide presentation. Another alternative format would be to create cards with the "imagine" verb phrases in one color and the "do" activity phrases in another color. Place the cards face down and allow students to select one "imagine" verb phrase and one "do" activity at random.

ID BOARD: IMAGINE + DO

1. Choose one of the *imagine* verbs from the left side of the board. Read the sentence with the verb as written, or complete it as directed by your teacher.
2. Next, choose one of the *do* activities from the right column. You may choose any of the options allowed by your teacher. Your *imagine* phrase does not have to be used with the *do* activity directly next to it.
3. Complete the assignment you have selected.

***Imagine* Verbs (Pick One)**	***Do* Activities (Pick One)**
Imagine . . .	Tell what will happen to . . .
Pretend . . .	Predict the outcome of . . .
Assume . . .	Explain . . .
If you were to change . . .	Create . . .
Suppose . . .	Draw a representation of . . .
Visualize . . .	Survey and summarize your findings . . .

***Imagine* Verbs (Pick One)**	***Do* Activities (Pick One)**
Make a guess about . .	Write a new ending for . . .
Picture . . .	Design . . .
Transform . . .	Compare . . .
Form a mental picture of . . .	Justify . . .
Think of . . .	Compare/contrast . . .
Consider . . .	Revise . . .

Advanced Mentoring for Advanced Learners

Strategy Target

- Instruction

Purpose

Mentoring is generally defined as a process of advising, training, supporting, and encouraging others. Usually, a mentor is older than his or her mentee. Although mentoring programs have been used in education for some time, mentoring advanced learners is most effective if the process is differentiated from typical mentoring.

Because advanced learners are a diverse population and because some specific groups have been underrepresented in gifted and talented programs, schools should consider focusing their mentoring on underserved and/or undersupported students. These might include students who are economically disadvantaged; racially, ethnically, or linguistically diverse students; female students whose interests lie in traditionally male fields; students who are gifted/talented but underachieving; and students who are gifted but also have a disability (i.e., twice-exceptional learners).

Process

To use the Advanced Mentoring for Advanced Learners strategy effectively, follow these steps:

1. First, review the Mentoring Checklist provided at the end of this section. This contains a list of basic steps that will help your school or district establish a mentoring program.
2. Write specific guidelines for your mentoring program. These should include everything discussed on the Mentoring Checklist, as well as:
   - an overview of your program;
   - names and contact information for those responsible;

- communication procedures;
- necessary paperwork, including timelines and forms;
- descriptions of the roles and responsibilities of school personnel, mentors, and mentees;
- safety and security measures;
- confidentiality terms and an explanation of other legal issues;
- a specific and clear explanation of the characteristics of advanced learners;
- a "Frequently Asked Questions" section to minimize misunderstandings;
- other information your program feels is appropriate.

3. Carefully select mentors and mentees. Consider qualities of each person. Generally, mentors should show interest in the process, commit to spending the required amount of time with his or her mentee, and demonstrate an ability to establish relationships with students who are highly advanced.
4. Because advanced learners often have specific areas of strength, selecting mentors whose educational and professional skills match the interests of the student should be helpful. It is also important to remember that students who are extremely advanced may already have mastered a lot of content but still benefit from mentoring in research, technical, and communication skills.
5. For specific relationships, consider interests and demographic variables as well. There is some limited support in the research for matching students and adults of similar racial, ethnic, linguistic, and cultural backgrounds (Liang, Tracy, Kauh, Taylor, & Williams, 2006; Sanchez & Colon, 2005), although each team should carefully consider these issues on a student-by-student basis.
6. After matching mentors and mentees, complete the information and orientation meeting suggested in the checklist. Ensure that both mentors and mentees understand the process and the expectations. Ask students to complete the Getting Started form provided at the end of the section and share information with their mentors.
7. Set timelines for mentoring sessions, journal entries, follow-up meetings, and other required documentation (templates for both student and mentor journals are provided at the end of the section).
8. Be prepared to problem solve and make adjustments as needed. Then get started and watch for positive progress.

ADVANCED MENTORING FOR ADVANCED LEARNERS MENTORING CHECKLIST

This checklist provides steps for setting up an effective mentoring program for advanced learners. After completing it and beginning the mentoring program, educators can check on the progress of mentor/mentee relationships by reviewing the Student Journal and Mentor Journal entries.

- ❑ Before implementing the mentoring program, contact community leaders, civic groups, businesses, nonprofits, and other organizations in the community. Explain the purpose of the program, enlist support, and establish a pool of mentor candidates. Be sure to explain the characteristics of students who are gifted and talented/advanced learners.
- ❑ After establishing a pool of potential mentors, conduct the appropriate background and reference checks for volunteers and mentors required by your school district and governmental jurisdiction.
- ❑ Select students for the mentoring program. Focus on students who have demonstrated characteristics of giftedness but who may not have strong support for their interests or talents. Also consider students who have special interests and skills that your school may not have the resources to nurture and support.
- ❑ Identify each individual student's interests and needs. Use the Advanced Mentoring Relationship: Getting Started form to help with this process.
- ❑ Match students with mentors. When matching students with mentors, consider which characteristics are the key variables. These could include demographic variables, interests, time available, and others.
- ❑ After mentors and mentees have been selected and matched, conduct an information and orientation session. Review all written information available about the mentoring program. At a minimum, a program description and mentoring guidelines should be provided.
- ❑ Establish the mentoring schedule for each student and his or her mentor. Also assign school personnel who will monitor the mentoring program and the specific relationships.
- ❑ Regularly review the entries in the student and mentor journals to ensure positive relationships and progress.
- ❑ If specific mentor-mentee situations do not work out, reassign mentors and mentees as needed.

ADVANCED MENTORING RELATIONSHIP: GETTING STARTED

Name: ____ Date: _________________

Your age: __________

What topics, subjects, or activities are you most interested in pursuing?

____

____

____

____

____

Would you like to work with a mentor? Yes No

If yes, what, in general, would you like to gain from the mentor/mentee relationship?

____

____

____

____

____

What are some specific goals you have?

____

____

____

____

____

After each mentoring session, you should complete an entry in your Student Journal.

Do you agree to do this? Yes No

ADVANCED MENTORING RELATIONSHIP: STUDENT JOURNAL

Your name: ______________________________

Your mentor's name: ______________________________

Date of mentoring session/meeting: ______________________________

What did you do during your mentoring session?

____

____

____

What did you discuss during your mentoring session?

____

____

____

Did your time with your mentor meet your expectations and goals? Explain.

____

____

____

What is your next step with your mentor?

____

____

____

Did you invest in the time with your mentor and give it your full attention, interest, and effort? Explain.

____

____

____

In general, how do you feel about the time spent with your mentor?

____

____

____

ADVANCED MENTORING RELATIONSHIP: MENTOR JOURNAL

Your name: ______________________________

Your mentee's name: ______________________________

Date of mentoring session/meeting: ______________________________

What did you and your mentee do during your mentoring session?

____

____

____

What did you discuss during your mentoring session?

____

____

____

Did your time with your mentee meet your expectations and goals? Explain.

____

____

____

What is your next step with your mentee?

____

____

____

Did your mentee invest in the time with you and give it his or her full attention, interest, and effort? Explain.

____

____

____

In general, how do you feel about the time spent with your mentee?

____

____

____

In-Class Acceleration

Strategy Target

- Instruction

Purpose

Most teachers who work with students identified as gifted/talented or advanced learners are familiar with the term "acceleration." Acceleration refers to the practice of presenting curriculum content earlier or at a faster pace.

Although acceleration used to refer to the practice of allowing students to skip grades, there are other ways to offer acceleration to students. If you take the approach that advanced learners are not always well matched for the grade-level curriculum that they are being taught, then acceleration makes a lot of sense. Students should not have to put in "seat time" when they have already mastered the material that is being taught. In addition, research supports acceleration for increasing the academic achievement of advanced learners (Rogers, 2002).

Process

To implement the In-Class Acceleration strategy, follow these steps:

1. Review the student's most recent academic achievement. This can include scores on summative assessments, in-class performance, diagnostic evaluations, formative assessments, and any sociocultural information that is available. Preassess the student on the content related to the unit/topic.
2. Have a discussion with the student about the acceleration process. Explain that acceleration involves not completing every assignment or activity that is provided in the class. Some units, lessons, or assignments will not be required.
3. Also explain that in lieu of the assignments that other students are doing, acceleration will entail other higher level work. This work may be enrichment that broadens

or deepens the topic or an extension that expands knowledge beyond the curriculum objectives. Either approach is acceptable and may be used.

4. To plan the acceleration with the student, use the In-Class Acceleration Plan provided at the end of this section. This checklist offers a wide range of ideas for acceleration. Selecting which ones to use may depend on the goals, objectives, and topics included in the curriculum.
5. After planning acceleration for the student, explain that he or she will still be required to complete assigned work, and much of it may be done independently, with technology, or at a higher grade or level.
6. Ask the student to monitor his or her progress and be very clear about expectations for independent work, including quality, timelines, and grading criteria.

IN-CLASS ACCELERATION PLAN

Name:____ Date: ________________

Goal/Objective/Topic: ____

Check each acceleration strategy that will be used. When assignments have been completed, self-evaluate and provide evidence to the teacher of satisfactory completion.

- ❑ Complete a web-based research project with specific sources. Present it to the class.
- ❑ Review vocabulary with the class at the beginning of the unit, and then move on to work detailed in a contract.
- ❑ Complete a special station.
- ❑ As assigned by your teacher, participate in instruction in a higher grade or a different class.
- ❑ Work with another student or a small group to complete enrichment or extension assignments.
- ❑ Complete a self-paced online course.
- ❑ Design your own independent study, get teacher approval, and check in at regular intervals.
- ❑ Enroll in advanced placement or concurrent enrollment classes.
- ❑ Test out of a class by taking the summative assessment before beginning. Instead, move on to higher level work as assigned by your teacher.
- ❑ If some material, but not all, is appropriate and needs to be learned, do what the teacher requires and skip the rest.
- ❑ Complete a project-based learning project to answer a driving question related to the unit of instruction.
- ❑ Work with a mentor to complete a special project.
- ❑ Complete a research project that answers a unique question about the topic or links it to other related topics.
- ❑ Create a portfolio of work on a specific topic by mutual agreement with your teacher. Use community resources, not just information provided at school.
- ❑ Complete a distance learning course through a local or national university.
- ❑ Do an internship with specific guidelines and criteria for completion.

REFERENCES

Berger, A. A. (1991). *Media analysis techniques.* Thousand Oaks, CA: Sage.

Buck Institute for Education. (2014). *PBL essential elements checklist.* Retrieved from http://bie.org/object/document/pbl_essential_elements_checklist

Drapeau, P. (2014). *Sparking student creativity.* Alexandria, VA: ASCD.

Dunn, J. (2012). 15 lesson plans for making students better online researchers. *Edudemic.* Retrieved from http://www.edudemic.com/students-better-online-researchers/

Heacox, D. (2009). *Making differentiation a habit: How to ensure success in academically diverse classrooms.* Minneapolis, MN: Free Spirit Publishing.

Hertz, M. B. (2012). Doing Internet research at the elementary level. *Edutopia.* Retrieved from http://www.edutopia.org/blog/elementary-research-mary-beth-hertz

Hudson, H. T. (2014). The 6 online research skills your students need. *Instructor.* Retrieved from http://www.scholastic.com/teachers/article/6-online-research-skills-your-students-need

Johnsen, S. K., Haensly, P. S., Ryser, G. R., & Ford, R. F. (2002). Changing general education classroom practices to adapt for gifted students. *Gifted Child Quarterly, 45*(1), 45–63.

Johnsen, S. K., Ryser, G. R., & Assouline, S. G. (2014). *A teacher's guide to using the Common Core State Standards with mathematically gifted and advanced learners.* Waco, TX: Prufrock Press.

Liang, B, Tracy, A., Kauh, T., Taylor, C., & Williams. L. (2006). Mentoring Asian and Euro-American college women. *Journal of Multicultural Counseling and Development, 24,* 243–254.

Mississippi State University. (2009). *Webb's depth of knowledge guide.* Retrieved from http://www.aps.edu/rda/documents/resources/Webbs_DOK_Guide.pdf

Reis, S. M., Burns, D. E., & Renzulli, J. S. (1992). *Curriculum compacting: The complete guide to modifying the curriculum for high-ability students.* Mansfield Center, CT: Creative Learning Press.

Renzulli, J. (1977). *The enrichment triad model: Guide for developing defensible programs for the gifted and talented.* Mansfield Center, CT: Creative Learning Press.

Renzulli, J. S., & Reis, S. M. (1998). Talent development through curriculum differentiation. *NASSP Bulletin, 82*(595), 61–74.

Rogers, K. (2002). Effects of acceleration in gifted learners. In M. Neihart, S. Reis, N. Robinson, & S. M. Moon (Eds.), *The social and emotional needs of gifted students: What do we know?* (pp. 3–13). Washington, DC: National Association for Gifted Children.

Sanchez, B., & Colon, Y. (2005). Race, ethnicity, and culture in mentoring relationships. In D. L. DuBois & M. J. Karcher (Eds.), *Handbook of Youth Mentoring* (pp. 191–204). Thousand Oaks, CA: Sage.

Scott, G., Leritz, L. E., & Mumford, M. D. (2004). The effectiveness of creativity training: A quantitative review. *Creativity Research Journal, 16*(4), 361–388.

Shaunessy, E. (1999). Questioning techniques in the gifted classroom. *Gifted Child Today,* 23(5), 14–21.

Sheffield, L. J. (2000). Creating and developing promising young mathematicians. *Teaching Children Mathematics,* 6(6), 416–419, 426.

Stanley, T. (2012). *Project-based learning for gifted students: A handbook for the 21st century classroom.* Waco, TX: Prufrock Press.

Tomlinson, C. A. (2014). *The differentiated classroom: Responding to the needs of all learners* (2nd ed.). Alexandria, VA: Association for Supervision and Curriculum Development.

Tomlinson, C. A., Brighton, C., Hertberg, H., Callahan, C. M., Moon, T. R., Brimijoin, K., Conover, L. A., & Reynolds, T. (2003). Differentiation instruction in response to student readiness, interest, and learning profile in academically diverse classrooms: A review of the literature. *Journal for the Education of the Gifted 27*(2/3), 119–145.

VanTassel-Baska, J., & Brown, E. F. (2007). Toward best practice: An analysis of the efficacy of curriculum models in gifted education. *Gifted Child Quarterly, 51*(4), 342–358.

ABOUT THE AUTHORS

Gail R Ryser, Ph.D., is director of the Testing, Research-Support, and Evaluation Center at Texas State University. She is an associate editor for *Gifted Child Quarterly.* She is the author of several tests and has written numerous articles related to gifted education, mathematics education, and measurement. She is a coauthor of a popular series of books, *Practical Ideas That Really Work,* which includes research-based instructional strategies for students with exceptionalities. She may be reached at gr16@txstate.edu.

Kathleen McConnell Fad, Ph.D., is an author and consultant from Austin, TX. Kathy's professional experience has spanned over 30 years as a general education teacher, special education teacher, university professor, author, and independent consultant. Kathy's specialty is designing practical, common sense strategies that are research based. Kathy has coauthored numerous books, articles, and assessment instruments, including the *Scales for Identifying Gifted Students* (SIGS). Kathy's professional development often relates to differentiated instructional strategies, collaboration, and RTI interventions that impact both academics and behavior. Kathy has a master's degree and Ph.D. in special education, as well as teaching and consulting experience in general education. She often works with beginning teachers and schools working to maintain effective student intervention teams and implement Tier 2 and Tier 3 academic or behavioral interventions. Kathy and a colleague, Paula Rogers, have a website with resources for educators: *Tools for Great Teachers,* which can be found at http://www.toolsforgreatteachers.com.